BEHIND THE CAMERA

James Cameron

Ron Howard

Spike Lee

George Lucas

Rob Reiner

Steven Spielberg

Rob Reiner

Joe Ferry

Chelsea House Publishers
Philadelphia

Frontis: Rob Reiner on set of *North.*

CHELSEA HOUSE PUBLISHERS

EDITOR IN CHIEF Sally Cheney
DIRECTOR OF PRODUCTION Kim Shinners
CREATIVE MANAGER Takeshi Takahashi
MANUFACTURING MANAGER Diann Grasse

STAFF FOR ROB REINER

ASSOCIATE EDITOR Ben Kim
PRODUCTION ASSISTANT Jaimie Winkler
PICTURE RESEARCHER Sarah Bloom
SERIES AND COVER DESIGNER Takeshi Takahashi
LAYOUT 21st Century Publishing and Communications, Inc.

©2002 by Chelsea House Publishers,
a subsidiary of Haights Cross Communications.
All rights reserved. Printed and bound in the United States of America.

http://www.chelseahouse.com

First Printing

1 3 5 7 9 8 6 4 2

Library of Congress Cataloging-in-Publication Data

Ferry, Joe, 1954–
   Rob Reiner / Joe Ferry.
      p. cm. — (Behind the camera)
Summary: A biography of the award-winning actor/director who became
well-known for his role in the popular television series, All in the Family.
Includes bibliographical references and index.
   ISBN 0-7910-6717-3
   1. Reiner, Rob—Juvenile literature. 2. Motion picture producers and
directors—United States—Biography—Juvenile literature. 3. Actors—
United States—Biography—Juvenile literature. [1. Reiner, Rob. 2. Actors
and actresses. 3. Motion picture producers and directors.] I.Title. II. Series.
PN1998.3.R435 F47 2002
791.43'0233'092—dc21

Table of Contents

1   All for the Family   7

2   In the Shadow of the Father   15

3   Meathead Arrives   25

4   Finding Direction   37

5   High Praise, Loud Critics   49

6   Meathead for President?   71

Chronology   82

Filmography   83

Major Awards   86

Further Reading   87

Bibliography   88

Websites   89

Index   90

Most people know Rob Reiner as a successful film director and former co-star of TV's *All in the Family*. But since 1994 Reiner has also been politically active in supporting childhood development and education programs.

Chapter 1

All for the Family

PROUD AS A new father, the head of the California Children and Families Commission was playing tour guide. He criss-crossed Los Angeles County, showing off programs that receive money from a state tax on tobacco products.

One stop on the tour was at a day-care center where workers were learning how to enrich their program with an early literacy curriculum for toddlers. Another was at an apartment in Long Beach, where a home health-care worker helped a recovered drug addict reconnect with her baby girl, who had been in foster care. He also spent time at a pre-K-to-12 school with a family medical clinic, day care and an adult education center on its campus. He strode across the blacktop, past beige bungalows, past the cafeteria, and the aroma of steamed green beans, and stopped at the health clinic, where a prenatal class was in session.

"We're talking about body changes," the instructor said. Then she interrupted the lecture to ask this bearded, bearish man for an autograph. "My kids won't believe I met Meathead today," she exclaimed.

It isn't the most flattering name to trail a man for more than 25 years. But his association with the character who Archie Bunker often argued with on the 1970s revolutionary sitcom *All in the Family* doesn't bother Rob Reiner. A convenient liberal target for bigoted Bunker, the role not only launched Reiner's career as a successful Hollywood actor and director but also allowed him to voice many of the views he shared with the character he played in the series. Both, for instance, believed that government should move more aggressively to correct social ills.

But while Meathead's political and philosophical rants are seen only on cable-TV reruns nowadays, Reiner has taken his act to the real world. He no longer merely talks about what the government should be doing. He is part of the government and he is doing something important.

Since 1999, Reiner has held an unpaid position chairing a California state commission dedicated to helping young children. He's also much wiser about what happens when an individual determined to ease social problems meets the reality of a slow-moving, unwieldy government bureaucracy.

For two years after the initiative passed in November 1998, Reiner stepped behind the camera only to produce educational videos for new parents. Essentially, the director of a string of hit movies put a successful Hollywood career on hold to wage an uphill fight to get the government to adequately fund early childhood development programs.

While movies may affect people's lives, they don't have the long-lasting, profound effect of a home-visit program, he believes.

Reiner's interest in a child's early development dated back more than 20 years to when his sister, Annie, a psychoanalyst, encouraged him to examine his formative years in analysis. After completing therapy, he wondered about the upbringing of kids who turned up on the 11 o'clock news as criminals. "You always see the same report," he said. "'He was a nice kid, so polite, I can't believe he would . . . ' I thought, 'Something's missing here.'"

After getting married for the second time in May 1989 and starting his own family, Reiner's concern for early childhood development was re-ignited. He invited experts to his home to educate him on the subject and was appalled to find out that only 10 percent of all children's funding is spent on them before they start school.

But it would be a few more years before his interest led to action. In 1994, he asked his assistant to call the office of Tipper Gore, wife of then Vice President Al Gore. He called her out of the blue, with no idea what he was doing. But he knew he needed help in generating support for his ideas.

Tipper Gore knew Reiner as a celebrity and as a reliable contributor to the Democratic Party, but she knew nothing of his interest in early childhood development. The two met, and soon Reiner was in touch with a network of experts, courtesy of Gore. He also read the Carnegie Corporation's "Starting Points" report, which summarized new findings about how an inadequate environment between birth and age three can compromise a child's brain development, and about the costs to society of ignoring that truth.

Reiner was astonished that the report had drawn so little attention. He decided he would share the information with anyone who would listen. Along with wife Michele Singer, a photographer, Reiner started the "I Am Your Child" foundation to spread the word. They produced a TV special on brain development and successfully lobbied the White House for a conference on the topic in 1997.

One of the people in the conference audience was former State Assemblyman Mike Roos of Los Angeles. Roos approached Reiner with the idea for Proposition 10, which they jointly introduced in California. The state allows private citizens to introduce ballot questions if they collect enough supporting signatures. Proposition 10 was an ambitious measure that sought to provide for the physical, mental, emotional and developmental needs of more than 500,000 children born in California every year.

Reiner fervently believes that if those needs are met in the first five years of life, children will be better prepared for school, which pays off not only by giving them better educational and work opportunities but also by diminishing the chances they will turn to crime, drug abuse or domestic violence.

As the campaign for Proposition 10 got underway, early polls indicated that 70 percent of voters favored the idea of a 50 cent tax on each package of cigarettes sold in California, with the $700 million raised going to early childhood development programs throughout the state. Then the tobacco industry, which opposed the tax, beefed up its advertising budget and began going after Reiner personally. In critical ads, they asked voters if they really wanted him, this creation of Hollywood, to take responsibility for raising their children.

In the mid-1990s Reiner and wife Michelle founded the "I Am Your Child" foundation, to focus more public attention on childhood development issues. Appearing before the House Human Resources Subcommitte in 1998, Reiner pressed for more awareness, funding, and government involvement.

In addition to his fame as Meathead, Reiner established himself as a premier Hollywood director with such box office hits as *This is Spinal Tap*, *Stand By Me*, *The Princess Bride*, and *When Harry Met Sally*. The ads suggested Reiner didn't know what he was talking about and suggested he only showed support to further his career.

"I don't know if Rob really realized when he got involved with a tobacco issue how they did things," said Alan Henderson, a professor of public health at Cal State Long Beach and author of the ballot language endorsing

In 1999, California governor Gray Davis named Reiner Chairman of the California Children and Families First Commission—testament to Reiner's commitment to improving standards of childhood development and education. Reiner was instrumental in the passage of Proposition 10, a state law that taxes cigarettes to pay for youth programs.

Proposition 10 for the voter handbook. "The attacks on him were relentless."

Support for the proposition began to slip, and then to fall dramatically. By the time the campaign entered its last month, Reiner was fearful of losing, exhausted and discouraged by the beating he was taking in the ads. Then Al Gore got involved and, as the former vice president remembered, "did everything I could do to help him pass it." Reiner was overjoyed by Gore's help. But the initiative was still in trouble.

On Election Day, returns late into the night showed the

measure failing. "It was horrible. Horrible!" Reiner remembers. But early in the morning, the tide slowly turned. By 3 A.M., the "yes" votes held a narrow lead. It was only two weeks later, after all the absentee ballots had been counted, that Reiner could finally exhale. Proposition 10 passed by less than half a percentage point.

Still, the battle wasn't over.

Four months later, the owners of a cigarette retail chain put Proposition 28 on the ballot, seeking to repeal the Proposition 10 tax. This time, 72 percent of California voters endorsed the tax. The law has also survived a state Supreme Court challenge on the grounds that it funds programs from a tax on an unrelated product.

With the victory finally assured, Reiner thought it was time to move on to something else. The idea, he said, was to pass Proposition 10 and let other people run the program.

But California Governor Gray Davis had other ideas and soon appointed Reiner to the state commission overseeing the program, a position he will hold until 2005. Then, perhaps, he will resume the successful Hollywood career that made possible his foray into government bureaucracy.

Reiner's exposure to the performing arts started early. Both father Carl and mother Estelle were in show business. Carl, a writer and comedian, helped usher in the Golden Age of TV with his work on *Your Show of Shows* and *The Dick Van Dyke Show*.

Chapter 2

In the Shadow of the Father

THE REINER SAGA began on March 6, 1945 when Rob was born into a family already heavily involved in show business. His father, Carl, was appearing at that time in a touring revue. His mother, Estelle, was an actress and entertainer. Already influenced by backstage babysitters, little Rob, allegedly cuter than one might today imagine compared to the burly, bearded bear of a man he is today, was being raised in the Bronx. Across the street—although he didn't know it at the time—lived a little girl named Penny Marshall.

As Rob grew up, things were always hopping in the Reiner household. Carl was writing and performing for *Your Show of Shows*, a popular weekly variety television show of the time. He and his colleagues, the likes of Mel Brooks, Sid Caesar, Neil Simon, and Imogene Coca, didn't know it then but they had practically invented the golden age of television. The gang would often gather at the Reiner apartment and Fire Island summerhouse, and Rob would listen while the witty grownups incessantly tried to make one another laugh.

Lucky kid? Maybe so. But it took Rob a lifetime to recover from being intimidated by the extraverts that surrounded him and to make his own career without the help of his famous father. It wasn't until he was 40 years old and recognized as one of the most talented movie directors in the world that Rob felt like he was his own man. "I think I'm finally coming out of adolescence," he said in a 1987 interview.

Despite the show business trappings, Rob didn't consider himself very different from other kids his age.

"I was very normal in my own mind," he said. "When you grow up as a kid, you don't think your household is any different from anyone else's household. You just assume this is the way everyone lives."

By age 6, Rob was hooked on storytelling. On Sunday mornings, Rob and his sister would run up two flights of stairs to his aunt's apartment where she would make pancakes and his uncle would tell stories. "He would put us in the stories," Reiner recalled. "It was the highlight of my week."

Recalling the moment when he first noticed that the nine-year-old Rob was funny, family friend Norman Lear said it occurred in 1956, when the Reiner and Lear families had neighboring cottages on New York's Fire Island and young Rob sat on the floor playing jacks with Lear's oldest daughter, Ellen.

"I said to Carl, 'He's hysterical,' and Carl said, 'What do you mean he's hysterical?' because a father doesn't see it that way," Lear said.

It was a perception by his father that bothers Reiner to this day, one that caused him many years of psychological pain and insecurity. It was tough for him to live in the shadow of a father who loved him dearly but couldn't see his son's unique abilities. When someone as visible and talented and successful as Carl Reiner doesn't give his child encouragement to move ahead in the business, it's an invitation to try another kind of career.

"That pretty much for most people I think would be enough to say, 'OK, I'm not going to be doing this now as my living,' you know, because whatever it is you're going to do, you want your father or your parents to encourage it," Rob said.

Nor did Rob always share his father's sense of fun. He was—and still is—much more serious, brooding, and quiet than his father. Carl Reiner's group of friends could all hold their own and trade shtick and make each other laugh for hours at a time. Even as an adult, Rob wouldn't fit into that kind of situation, but when he was a kid, Reiner would never fit in.

Rob remembers people telling him over and over again as a youngster how great his dad was. He never felt like he could measure up to that kind of reputation. He remembers visiting the set of *The Dick Van Dyke Show*—a remarkably popular weekly television situation comedy of the 1960s—and sitting behind his father's

Unlike his father Carl (seen here accepting two Emmy Awards for *The Dick Van Dyke Show*), Rob was shy and introspective as a kid. It would be years before Carl would see his son's talent and encourage him to pursue it.

desk, looking at all the Emmy Awards and feeling very inadequate. He was thinking that he should be able to write for the show, just like his father, even though he was only 13 years old. He couldn't, of course, and it was very frustrating. Rob was actually jealous of his father.

Not surprisingly, Reiner described himself as an incredibly shy, introspective kid. It was difficult for him to feel he had a place in the house because his father was so much larger than life. He couldn't figure out how to fit in.

"I don't think he quite understood how I was as a person," Rob said of his father. "He never thought I had a sense of humor, never thought I was funny."

Soon, though, the Reiner's moved on from New York City, first to suburban New Rochelle, where dad seemed like any other suburban commuter—except that he worked only 39 weeks a year on a hit TV show—then in 1959 to Beverly Hills.

Rob spent his vacation afternoons watching his father put together *The Dick Van Dyke Show*. He began to understand what audiences considered funny.

The showbiz bug bit him hard. By 12th grade, Reiner discovered the drama department at his high school and felt comfortable on stage. Encouraged by his mother, Rob spent the summer working in Bucks County, Pennsylvania painting sets and building scenery for a theater.

In 1963, Rob did a summer production of his father's play *Enter Laughing*. The audience loved it but Rob knew his father hated it, even though he tried to hide the fact. Rob found out later from another actor that his father was trying to figure out a way to get his son to give up being in show business. He was applying rules to his son that he wouldn't have applied to any other 18-year-old.

A year later, however, Carl Reiner began to recognize his son's talent. Rob directed a product of Sartre's *No Exit* in Beverly Hills at the Roxy Theater. Afterward, Carl Reiner came backstage, looked his son straight in the eye and said: "That was good."

The next day, Carl repeated his praise, telling Rob in no uncertain terms that he had the ability to do whatever he wanted to do in show business. It was the first time Rob had received that sort of positive encouragement from his father.

After high school, Rob entered the University of California at Los Angeles but got kicked out for skipping too many classes. Then he was called to take a physical before being drafted into the service. The war in Vietnam was just starting to escalate.

Instead of serving in the military, however, Rob got a note from a psychiatrist that said: "He's crazy and would not be helpful to us in Vietnam." The note earned him a deferment, which was fortunate because he didn't want to go to Canada to avoid the draft and was prepared to go to jail if necessary. The worst thing about the war? "It made people who were patriotic feel they were not patriotic," he said. "You were told you weren't a patriot because you didn't want to go and kill people whose country we had no business being in the first place. That, to me, was the biggest crime of all."

After UCLA, Reiner began to spend most of his time around other comedy-struck kids. The humor was centered in a small circle of Beverly Hills High School buddies, notably the class cutup, Albert Brooks; a scrawny would-be actor named Ricky Dreyfuss; and another famous TV personality's son, Larry (son of Joey) Bishop. They constantly fantasized about fame and fortune in comedy.

The guys, along with a few other intrepid souls, formed a comedy troupe called The Session. Sometimes, the gags were very broad (a TV-game show take-off called "Let's Watch a Death," involving the electrocution of a midget, was a big favorite). But sometimes, the comedy was lost on the audience.

By age 18, Rob began to have some success in stand-up comedy. Performing in the late 1960s with an improvisational group called The Committee (seen here in a reunion photo), Rob worked with future TV stars David Ogden Stiers (*M*A*S*H*), Peter Bonerz (*The Bob Newhart Show*) and Howard Hesseman (*WKRP in Cincinnati* and *Head of the Class*).

With some successful forays into stand-up comedy, Rob got noticed. He began appearing in The Committee, another improvisational group that, in the late 1960s, was as close to the cutting edge of music as of comedy. He would hang out with the likes of Mama Cass, Harvey

Brooks and Steve Miller. Occasionally, Janis Joplin would join the troupe on its San Francisco stage.

By the time he turned 19, Reiner began to land a few small acting jobs, mostly to play a zoned-out, long-haired hippie on some of the most un-hip shows on television at the time. He appeared on episodes of *The Beverly Hillbillies*, *Gomer Pyle USMC*, and *That Girl*. Then he did a show called *The Mothers-in-Law*. He was playing—what else?—a hippie, and they were doing a run-through before the final taping. He had this tiny little scene, and, in the middle of the run-through, he came up with a funny line and just threw it in. He got a big laugh but the director (Desi Arnaz) didn't like it because he wasn't following the script.

Arnez was furious. Reiner was afraid that he had upset a famous actor and director. Arnaz invited him off to the side of the set to talk privately. With everyone watching, Arnaz screamed at Reiner for ruining the rehearsal. Rob tried to make amends. "Listen, let's just forget about it. It's only a five-line part. You can get someone else," Reiner told Arnaz.

But Arnaz refused. "No, amigo, no," Reiner recalled Arnaz saying. "Don't worry about it, amigo. We'll fix it."

But eventually Reiner said they would be better off with another actor. He left and they found another actor to do the part.

But that night, on Rona Barrett's *News from Holly-wood* television show, a report aired that described a different series of events. "Rob Reiner, actor, hippie-psychedelic son of actor Carl Reiner, got into a fight with Desi Arnaz on the *Mothers-in-Law* set and—whoops—the bearded bad boy walked off."

Rona Barrett was a very big Hollywood gossip reporter

at the time and Reiner loved the way she described him. He thought it was amusing. "I just remember hearing that phrase and liking it so much: hippie-psychedelic son. Bearded-bad boy."

Rob first entered American living rooms in 1970, playing Michael Stivic (or "Meathead") in the successful TV show *All in the Family*. What Rob thought would be a one-season diversion ended up lasting eight years.

Chapter 3

Meathead Arrives

REINER'S MOST IMPORTANT career break came in the spring of 1968, when the Smothers Brothers hired him as a writer on their popular weekly television show. He was performing with The Committee in Los Angeles when Tommy Smothers, who was producing *The Glen Campbell Show*, happened to see him on working on stage. Smothers liked what he saw and hired Reiner and fellow-writer/performer Carl Gottlieb. They worked for the Campbell show the rest of that season and joined Tommy and Dick Smothers when their show started up in the fall for its first and only season.

The big break came along at an opportune time for Reiner. He was feeling confused about his place in the world and concerned about his professional future. The job was a wake-up call to reality. For the first time, he went from being the kid of the household to entering the adult world. It was the first time he truly realized that he wouldn't be able to lean on his parents forever.

Teamed with funnyman Steve Martin, who would later become a star with *Saturday Night Live*, Reiner encountered some frustrating moments early on. They wrote a couple of funny sketches but, because they were the youngest writers on the staff, had difficulty getting them on the air.

"When you're young, people try to slough you off, push you aside. It was very frustrating," Reiner said.

Soon after *The Smothers Brothers Show* was cancelled, the opportunity to audition for a revolutionary new weekly television series presented itself. Created by old family friend Norman Lear, *All in the Family* was an adaptation of a popular British comedy series called *Till Death Do Us Part*. It featured a bigoted, homophobic, conservative New Yorker named Archie Bunker (played by the late Carroll O'Connor), who shared his unique view of life with those closest to him: wife Edith (played by Jean Stapleton), daughter Gloria (Sally Struthers) and son-in-law Mike (Meathead) Stivic.

The show was one of the biggest hits in television history. According to *The Wall Street Journal*, *All in the Family* was watched regularly by nearly one-third of all Americans in its heyday. As a series, it remained secure among the top 10 shows for eight seasons and was the top-rated show for five consecutive seasons. Before its final season, on a per-episode basis, *All in the Family* had delivered six of the top 50 highest-rated programs of all time.

Reiner tried out for the role of Meathead twice and got rejected both times. On the third try, he passed and was given the part. Struthers was chosen to play Rob's wife, winning her role over Penny Marshall, the same little-known actress who used to live across from Reiner in the Bronx.

Reiner admitted he auditioned for the part only because he was convinced it wouldn't last a season. He thought it would be a fun but short-lived job. Eight years later he was still doing the Meathead role and trying to buy his way out of the contract. He loved the show but needed to get on with his life and career.

When he took the role of Mike Stivic, Reiner worried about getting sidetracked because his real interest was in writing, directing, and producing. It turned out to be the best kind of side-tracked. He learned how to structure stories, what worked and didn't work with an audience because they filmed in front of a live audience.

"I used to make a joke that no matter what accomplishments I had I would always be called Meathead," Reiner said. "I could win the Nobel Prize and the headline would be 'Meathead Wins Nobel.'"

Reiner felt a certain kinship with the evolution of his character on *All in the Family*. They both went through a similar transition over the years, starting out idealistically and then, as they gained responsibility with a baby and a job, began swinging toward the center. As most people do, they began accepting certain realities of life.

Reiner never wanted to do a TV series, either. He didn't want to work for five years making a whole career out of playing one character. The only thing that attracted him to

At the time, *All in the Family* was unlike any other TV show, with politically charged scripts that let Reiner's character challenge the bigoted views of the show's lead character, Archie Bunker (played by Carroll O'Connor).

All in the Family was the script he read. "I said, 'Wow, this is unlike anything that's ever been on television, and if I have a chance to be part of it, I want to,'" he recalled in a 1985 interview with *Playboy*.

Reiner expected the show to last 13 weeks and then go off the air. He didn't think the American public would accept a show that routinely made fun of blacks, Hispanics, Catholics, Jews and homosexuals. Boy, was he wrong!

The show debuted in the spring of 1970, but it didn't really catch on with audiences until the summer when the original 13 episodes were shown in reruns.

By the second year, the show was a hit and the stars, including Reiner, were hot commodities. For Reiner, it was exciting to be part of something that was so talked about, something that had so much impact on the American people. By the third season, however, Reiner felt some of the excitement starting to wear off. As expected, he was disheartened by the prospect of playing the same character for years on end.

In the fourth year of the series, however, Reiner made peace with himself and his career aspirations. He promised himself he would make the best of it and get something out of being on the show. The last fours years were wonderful because Reiner viewed it as though he was in school going through a valuable learning experience. "I thought, 'I'm learning what this is all about,'" he said.

That was because Lear and O'Connor set up ground rules that allowed the co-stars to have creative input into the series. Reiner was involved in helping structure the stories, in rewriting scripts, in editing—all the things that made the program. "If I had just had to do my part as an actor, go in every week and play the part, I think I would have been unhappy," he said.

Even as an actor, Reiner was always more aware of everybody else on stage, or if he was doing *All in the Family*, he was aware of where all the cameras were, where the other actors were, the audience. He was always more interested in the script than he was in his own performance, which is not such a great way to approach your acting job.

"Just about everything I've learned in making films I learned in the course of *All in the Family*: what audiences laugh at, how to structure a play. Because to me, TV and film is theater," he said.

All in the Family was a show without big egos and it taught Reiner a valuable lesson: that actors, writers and directors must work together to serve the final product. The show was a pure example of that kind of philosophy.

Some people claimed *All in the Family* was responsible for some measure of social change, in that it exposed bigotry and hate as little more than empty rhetoric. However, Reiner said the show's most significant contribution was in allowing a realistic portrait of people on television.

"Its impact was on people, and that's what theater is all about," he said. "To me, *All in the Family* was good theater."

As *All in the Family* zoomed in the ratings, Rob married Penny Marshall, his former childhood neighbor. The couple met at Barney's Beanery, a popular hangout bar on Santa Monica Boulevard. Joplin was a frequent visitor, as were Jack Nicholson and Harry Dean Stanton. Reiner was in the bar one day with some friends when Marshall stopped by with a group of her friends.

They had been acquaintances for several years but had not dated each other at all. The more time they spent together, however, the closer they became. Finally, they decided to get married on April 10, 1971.

"It was the next logical step," said Reiner. "I'd just turned 24. We'd been living together for a year and a half, we were getting along well, and we thought it was the next thing to do."

The wedding ceremony was held in the backyard of Reiner's parents' house. About 100 people showed up and they ordered $1,000 worth of takeout food from a Chinese restaurant to feed the guests. They improvised their vows, had their friends run the ceremony, and made sure a judge was on hand to keep everything legal.

In 1971 Rob married Penny Marshall (front left). Five years later, Penny's hit show *Laverne & Shirley* would knock Reiner's *All in the Family* out of the top ratings spot. Marshall's sitcom capitalized on the 1950s nostalgia craze set off by the film *American Graffiti* and TV show *Happy Days*.

For the first five years of their marriage, with *All in the Family* and Rob picking up Emmy Award after Emmy Award, Penny Marshall Reiner looked for steady work. When *Laverne & Shirley* made its debut in 1976, the show not only made Penny as big a TV star as her husband, it knocked his program out of the top ratings slot. For the next three seasons, Rob and Penny were a couple like George Burns and Gracie Allen for the seventies—only on separate channels.

But from the time Rob finished the final season on *All in the Family* in 1978, things started to fall apart for him, both personally and professionally. After eight years of doing a successful show, he began to believe that nothing bad could happen to him. When the show was canceled, Reiner was offered what he described as an enormous amount of money to appear in a spin-off. Instead, he turned it down and spent four years trying to answer the calling he felt was his all along.

Reiner and partner Phil Mishkin wrote and performed some well-received stage works, while churning out gags for everything from a Robert Young TV special to an Andy Griffith series called *Headmaster*.

Reiner also signed a production deal with ABC, but his two main projects—an ambitious comedy series about immigrants called *Free Country* and a satire program called *The TV Show*—died quickly in the midst of a network-management shakeup and disputes over censorship. The experience left him bitter and frustrated.

Reiner believed *Free Country* would have been one of the most innovative TV series ever created. It was basically a Jewish version of *Roots*, the popular mini-series about the history of an African-American family. Reiner thought the networks were not too thrilled about putting on a show about Jews.

"To be fair to them, though, they have a constituency out there that they have to program for," he said. "Shows like *Happy Days* were very big and successful then."

At the same time, Reiner began drifting apart from his wife. Part of the problem was *Laverne & Shirley* was still a big hit while Rob scrambled for work. Penny was the one getting all the attention and bringing home a big paycheck.

"I think any man would be lying if he said it wouldn't be an ego blow to see his wife making more money than he was or working when he was not," Reiner said.

After playing the role of supporting his wife's career ambitions for several years, Reiner suddenly wasn't doing that job. This time, he looked to Marshall for emotional support but she was too consumed with her own problems with the show to be of any help.

"I was thinking, 'I'm not getting anything here, I'm suffering, I'm not working and I don't have anybody around supporting me," he said.

Reiner hated *Laverne & Shirley* and didn't hesitate to tell his wife that he didn't think the show was very intelligent. In most cases, Penny thought Rob didn't like her performance. Looking back, Reiner said he understands why his wife got angry.

"You want your spouse to be supportive and on your side," he said. "She wanted me to just love what she was doing. And the fact was that I didn't."

In 1979, the couple divorced. For several years afterward, Reiner said he lived "a 24-hour horror show." He had no work and no marriage. "I cried quite a bit," he said. "There was an air of desperation about me for a lot of years."

Competition with his wife wasn't the only problem Reiner faced during those years. Living up to his father's reputation was just as difficult, if not more so. Being funny was something he felt he had to do. He did it, but there

Reiner didn't like Marshall's show *Laverne & Shirley*. And while the show soared in the ratings, Reiner's career drifted. Hard times continued for Rob when the couple divorced in 1979.

were times her felt uncomfortable being funny just to be competitive or to be accepted.

Unlike his father, who loves to perform, Rob never got a sense of satisfaction from being the center of attention. He remembers as a youngster walking down the street in New York with his father, who would suddenly start singing at the top of his lungs.

"Of course, everybody would look," Rob recalled. "And I'd be hiding my face, going, 'C'mon dad, please!'"

While he likes and needs some attention, Rob said his natural state is not jumping up in front of people and performing. A lot of what he did in his acting career was a way to show his father that he was capable of being a performer. It was only as he got older that Rob didn't feel that need as intensely.

Being the son of a famous performer was a double-edged sword for Reiner. While it opened doors to opportunities he might not otherwise have had, it also meant those doors would close quicker than they would for anybody else if he didn't measure up right away. People would be set to knock him down or say he was not as good as his father.

"Certainly, it is much more difficult getting there in the first place if you're not connected," he said. "But you can't sneak in the back door, hone your craft, and fail a little more easily until you're ready."

Reiner never felt guilty of taking advantage of his connections, mostly because there was always so much pressure on him to perform. People made comparisons to his father. Ever if those expectations weren't as great as his own, people always had preconceived notions about how he would be and what he should be doing.

After *All in the Family* ended and his divorce was finalized, Reiner decided to get his life in order. While he never wanted to be alone, Reiner said those years of being single allowed him to become comfortable being on his own, as a person and as a creative force.

Rob's first foray into film directing came with the 1982 rock documentary satire of fictional band "Spinal Tap." Contributions from Chris Guest, Michael McKean, Harry Shearer, Fred Willard, Billy Crystal, and Fran Drescher helped make the film a cult classic.

Chapter 4

Finding Direction

EVEN AS HE was starring in *All in the Family*, Reiner knew all along that his future would involve directing Hollywood films. And an obscure concept for a "mockumentary" (or mock documentary) about a non-existent rock and roll band would prove to be the perfect vehicle.

Over the years *This is Spinal Tap* has gained a cult following of faithful fans. In fact, a special DVD edition was released in 2002 to commemorate the 20th anniversary of the original release. But initially, making the movie—Reiner's first as director—was an intimidating prospect. While Reiner had a general idea of the kind of movie he wanted, there was nothing even approaching a script. The actors were expected to improvise most of their lines.

"I was a nervous wreck," he said. ""Because not only had I never done this before but we didn't have a script."

Close friend Billy Crystal said Reiner did a remarkable job getting the actors in the right frame of mind to portray their characters realistically.

"Real moments weren't people trying to do jokes," he said. "It was people just being naturally funny."

The idea behind *This is Spinal Tap*, a satire of everything pretentious and just plain phony about the 1980's rock scene, had been kicking around for quite some time. The problem was that Hollywood's moguls found the concept of an improvised, pseudo-documentary about a mythical heavy-metal band hard to fathom—or finance. It took Reiner four-and-a-half years of relentless hustling for the deal to be consummated because he couldn't find anyone to take him seriously.

Early in the process, Reiner and his partners put together a little 20-minute product reel that was a demonstration of the kind of satire they wanted to do. They arranged a screening at Columbia Pictures and none of the executives laughed. The lights went up when the mini-movie was over and they said: "Well, that's interesting. We'll think about it."

It was right on the cusp of time in which people who came out of television were thought to be pariahs. TV actors couldn't just go into features. It's different today, when Hollywood is practically begging high-profile television stars to be in movies.

Reiner eventually sold *Spinal Tap* to AVCO/Embassy but then Norman Lear, of all people, and a partner bought the studio. Reiner was sure the project would be scuttled but, instead, it was Lear who championed the studio's involvement with *Spinal Tap*.

In addition to directing the film, Reiner also played a major role in *Spinal Tap*. He appeared as Marti DiBergi, the young filmmaker who sets out to capture "the sights, the sounds, and the smells" of the workhorse British rock band. The film—humorous, shocking and completely made up—follows the band on its first U.S. tour in six years.

The movie is presented much like a typical concert film, along the lines of U2's *Rattle and Hum* or Madonna's *Truth or Dare*. Concert highlights are mixed with band interviews and glimpses into the lives of the band members backstage and on the road.

But while most concert films capture their worthy subjects at the peak of their popularity or during a triumphant reunion tour, *This is Spinal Tap* presents a second-rate band made up of aging members who are desperately trying to cling onto what little fame they used to have.

"Their appeal is becoming more selective," band manager Ian Faith tells DiBergi in the film, explaining why the band has been downgraded to performing in increasingly smaller venues and is forced to endure the cancellation of several shows. When the group plays the last show of its U.S. tour at a theme park, billed under a puppet show, the audience realizes that the band has sunk just about as low as it can go.

When *The Sure Thing*, a gentle romantic comedy about two collegians reminiscent of the classic romantic comedies of the 1950s, opened strongly in March 1985, Reiner proved that *Spinal Tap* was no fluke. In some ways, *The Sure Thing*, starring John Cusack and Daphne Zuniga as a couple forced to travel cross-country together, was a

Reiner followed *This is Spinal Tap* with the romantic comedy *The Sure Thing*, starring John Cusack and Daphne Zuniga. TV producer Norman Lear agreed to bankroll the film, even though he didn't like the script. The gamble paid off, and Reiner established himself as a director.

backlash against the teen exploitation films that were so popular in the mid-1980s. Reiner's goal was to produce a good movie that treated young people with some respect and showed that they had feelings that were just as deep and meaningful as anyone else. At first, he was worried because the movie didn't have car crashes, nudity or food fights. Basically, it was as simple love story about two characters who are on-screen for practically the whole movie. Reiner wondered whether audiences would sit still for such a movie.

Lear, who provided the financing for *This is Spinal Tap*, actually didn't like the script for *The Sure Thing* at all. He told Reiner in no uncertain terms that he didn't think it was funny. The opinion hurt Reiner, who respected Lear so much. He was the one man—other than his father—that Rob could say he loved. Finally, Lear put his faith in Reiner's judgment and talent as a director and agreed to bankroll the film.

Actor John Cusack, who played the male lead in *The Sure Thing*, said that Reiner's working style on the set was to create an atmosphere where the actors could thrive in their roles. He called Reiner the most passionate director he has ever worked with. For a young actor starting out in his career, it was a valuable experience for Cusack.

"He wants his actors to take chances and he basically will do anything to get you where he wants you to be," Cusack said. "You can always put it up against other acting experiences and you know that's the way it's supposed to be when it works."

The commercial and critical success of his second movie allowed Reiner to stop being a fanatical competitor, on the field as well as on the screen. That was never more evident than in his demeanor on a baseball field one day.

Reiner had played Little League baseball and later, played in softball leagues from the age of 24 until he was 29 and again from 33 to 38. He hit long balls in five annual actors-versus-sportswriters baseball games in Dodger Stadium.

Then came the moment of truth in his ball-playing life. It was a Valley League softball championship game in 1985. It was the last game of the season, the bottom of the tenth inning of a tie game. The rival team was at bat with two outs and runners are first and second base. Reiner was playing first base for the Coney Island Whitefish. His good buddy, Billy Crystal, was playing second.

Standing at first base, with the game on the line, Reiner suddenly realized he was bored. As he wondered what he was doing there, a grounder went by him, allowing the winning run to score.

"I didn't care," he said.

Reiner realized he didn't want to play ball any more. The thrill was gone. He hasn't played since.

"Your priorities shift," he said.

After *The Sure Thing*, Reiner produced *Stand by Me*, which starred four 12-year-old boys and was produced for less than $6 million. Based on a Stephen King story called "The Body," it grossed more than $53 million domestically at the box office and won Reiner a best-director nomination from the Directors Guild of America. The movie also received an Oscar nomination for best adapted screenplay of a novel.

Stand By Me, the story of young boys coming of age in the 1950s, was the most important film for Reiner up to that point because it was an attempt to do something totally unlike what his father would do. It was scary for Reiner because he was going out on his own.

"I felt like I was taking first step in my life toward breaking away from my father in a very significant way," he said.

Even though *This is Spinal Tap* was not the kind of film Carl Reiner would have made, it was a satire, which was his father's forte and Rob was raised on it. Carl Reiner even did a skit in the 1950s called "The Three Haircuts," a parody of the rock bands of the era. The satirical connection between father and son was there.

The fact that the tone of *Stand By Me* was so far from anything his father had done—and was so connected to Rob's personality—made a resounding statement. "It became my own rite of passage," Rob said.

Based on Stephen King's story "The Body," Reiner's film *Stand By Me* follows four 12-year-old boys as they journey to find a dead body along a railroad track. The low-budget coming-of-age film scored a big hit with audiences, earning the movie an Oscar nomination for best adaptation.

Actor Corey Feldman credited Reiner with making a film that people could relate to.

"Everyone can remember when they were 14 and they had their best friends," he said. "It brought back memories of their childhood. Rob really captured that precise moment in time when you cross the imaginary line from childhood to adulthood."

With a movie focused so heavily on four young actors, Reiner knew he couldn't approach their performance in a traditional way. While they had good acting instincts he knew could be tapped into, they didn't have the experience that an older actor can draw on.

For three weeks before the film began rehearsals, Reiner conducted his own acting classes for the boys. What he tried to do was give them some sense of stage discipline, an improvisational method of connecting with each other so they could bounce back and forth among one another in a scene. "It helped a lot when we began to shoot," Reiner said.

The positive emotional response by the public to *Stand By Me* boosted Reiner's self-esteem. He was shocked, for example, to see a Budweiser commercial during the Super Bowl one year in which two guys are walking arm-in-arm down a railroad track, just about re-enacting a scene from the movie. It proved that the film had worked its way into the fabric of society.

But *Stand By Me* was not without its difficult moments. Two days before they were to start principal photography, Coca-Cola decided it didn't want to go ahead with the project. Reiner was in Oregon with the four youngsters ready to start work on the film.

"We had everything, a whole crew, a cast, everything was there," Reiner said.

Once again, Lear found out what was happening and offered to foot the bill for production. To Reiner, it was a godsend, the only way he could get to do the movie.

When the movie was completed, every major studio refused distribution except Columbia, which had already rejected the film in script form. They had told Reiner they didn't want anything to do with the picture. But to Lear and Reiner's surprise, when the completed picture was screened

Peter Falk as the grandfather in *The Princess Bride*. Although others thought that the characters of the grandfather and his grandchild should be left out of the movie, Reiner insisted that they remain, as he felt the characters were integral to the movie.

for Columbia executives as a last resort, studio president Guy McElwaine loved it. Columbia picked up the movie.

For Reiner, *Stand by Me* was about himself, even though it featured 12-year-old boys.

"It was all about the beginnings of learning to like yourself, beginning to accept yourself, with the help of good friends who could maybe help you validate yourself by seeing what was good in you," he said.

With a price tag of $17 million, *The Princess Bride*, released in 1988, was Reiner's most expensive movie to date. It was also the biggest test he had faced after leaving behind his "Meathead" character. The movie is based on the 1973 novel written by Academy Award winner William Goldman for his two daughters as a fairy tale that leaves out the dull parts. In a tongue-in-cheek preface, Goldman attributes the book to another writer, takes credit only for making the story shorter, and interrupts periodically to explain what is left out and why.

Ironically, when he finished the book, Goldman sent it to Carl Reiner, thinking he might want to do something with it for the screen. Knowing Rob was a huge fan of Goldman's works, Carl passed the book onto his son.

Rob, who was in his early 20s at the time, was floored when he read the book. Twelve years later, Rob was sitting around with good friend Andrew Schienman wondering about the next project he should undertake. He decided that it made sense to make a movie based on a popular book. Rob's favorite book? *The Princess Bride*, of course.

At his first meeting with Goldman, Reiner got a sense of how serious the task of adapting the book would be.

"The first thing he said was '*The Princess Bride* is my favorite thing I've ever written,'" Reiner recalled. "'It's my baby. I want it on my tombstone. What are you going to do with it?' It was like a real challenge. I didn't want to destroy his baby."

In Reiner's adaptation of the book, a wise and crusty grandfather, played by Peter Falk, reads the book aloud to his 9-year-old grandson, who is sick in bed with the flu. The story is interrupted several times by the young boy when he's embarrassed by a kissing scene or worried for the safety of the hero or anxious for the villain to be punished.

Reiner managed to tell a fairytale love story while at the same time showing the advancement of the relationship between the grandfather and grandson. At the beginning, the kid is annoyed when his grandfather shows up because he'd rather be playing video games alone. But as he gets drawn into the story, the youngster gets closer to his grandfather. At the last moment, the boy invites his grandfather to come back and read to him again the next day.

During both the writing and filming of *The Princess Bride*, Reiner took some heat for having the boy interrupt the action to say what someone in the audience might be thinking. He was asked repeatedly to leave the kid and the grandfather out of the movie completely. Reiner refused.

"To me, they sanction the story, allow the story to take place," he said. "Because, if we didn't have them, then all you've got is a fairy tale story."

For some reason, several directors expressed interest in making the movie but backed out at the last minute. Even Robert Redford, who had a yen to play Westly, the farm boy in the story, turned down an opportunity to direct the movie.

"This movie didn't not get made for 14 years for no reason," Reiner noted gleefully.

Largely faithful to the book, the movie is about a milk-maid who becomes the Princess Buttercup, the farm boy she loves, an evil prince, a giant and a Spanish swordsman avenging his father's death in a land that takes its fairytale quality seriously—but not much else.

Reiner's 1990 romantic comedy *When Harry Met Sally* was the first produced by his own company, Castle Rock Entertainment. The film starred Billy Crystal and Meg Ryan and drew from Reiner's own dating experiences.

Chapter 5

High Praise, Loud Critics

BY THE END of 1990, Reiner was riding a wave of improbable success behind the camera that still had not reached its peak. His next movie, *When Harry Met Sally*, starred Meg Ryan and Billy Crystal. It was an unfashionably talky romantic comedy about friends who become lovers. It also turned out to be his biggest hit yet, grossing close to $100 million, and earned Reiner a nomination for Best Director from the Director's Guild of America as well as an Oscar nomination for best original screenplay.

For Reiner, it was the fifth movie he directed but the first to be produced by his own company, Castle Rock Entertainment, which he formed in 1987. It represented his first undis-guised attempt to address adult issues, specifically the difficulties faced by men and women trying to establish friendships amid the quicksand of sexual desire.

Having borrowed heavily from his own raw experiences as a divorced man, Reiner, who by then had remarried, figured that older audiences would sympathize with the obsessively verbal characters—but what of the teenagers in the audience? Would they respond to a movie that offers melancholy jokes about inconvenient ex-wives, untrustworthy old boyfriends and clashing tastes in interior decorating?

The project, which had matured over four years, had grown out of a let's-all-do-lunch meeting between Reiner, producer Andrew Schienman and writer Nora Ephron. During the requisite small talk, Ephron began interviewing the two men about their troubles being single.

Following his divorce from Marshall, Reiner wasn't at all thrilled by his re-entry into the single scene. So he threw out some of his pet theories. One of his favorites concluded that men and women can be best friends, but only with some sort of sexual something or other being thrown into the mix. The sexuality is always there, he suggested, and it's either acted upon or not acted upon. If it's not acted upon, one or the other or both will find someone else they can be sexually involved with, and once they are, the friendship will eventually decay.

Ephron, a longtime observer of the battle of the sexes, was inclined to agree, and she began fashioning a screenplay while Reiner was busy filming *The Princess Bride*. It was only several drafts later, with Ephon having explored so many of Reiner's true-life confessions, that the director could claim the movie was autobiographical in spirit if not in fact—that the collaborators turned to the matter of casting.

Impressed by Reiner's own script readings, Ephron said she went through the entire casting process hoping that Reiner would come to his senses and play the part.

But the balding Reiner had no interest in playing the young Harry. For a while, he was leaning toward Dreyfus, his old high school pal, but he argued for script changes showing other aspects of Harry's life, at which Reiner balked. Eventually, after considering a long list of actors, Reiner finally made the call to another friend, Billy Crystal.

It turned out to be a stroke of genius. That the part of Harry Burns afforded him such an opportunity was less a tribute to Reiner's foresight, because the part was not specifically written for Crystal, than it was a measure of the psychic connection between the two collaborators.

And for that connection, Lear deserved credit. He was the one who first cast Crystal as Reiner's best friend in an episode of *All in the Family*. Crystal vividly remembered his first meeting with Reiner, who proved to be far more clever than the lumbering character he played in the show.

"I was on the set," Crystal recalled. "Rob came out and said, 'I saw you on the Cosell show (Howard Cosell's variety series). It was good."

Crystal was nervous and he said something stupid. "Yeah, it was friendly," he told Reiner.

For the rest of the day, Crystal kept thinking about what a stupid thing he had said. But as the week progressed, he could see that Reiner was clearly the smartest one at the table. He would rewrite parts of the script, and Crystal could see he was really good at it.

It wasn't until about 1982 that the two men realized how deeply attuned they were. One day, they were sitting at Crystal's house talking about how depression manifests itself physically.

A long-time friend of Reiner's, comedian Billy Crystal proved a huge help in creating *When Harry Met Sally*. Although the film drew some negative reviews, it proved a hit with audiences.

Reiner described headaches that felt like rubber bands across his eyes. Crystal compared his to a drummer tuning up on the back of his neck. Suddenly, the two men were in hysterics.

"It was two guys talking to each other like I don't think guys talk to each other," Crystal said.

Eventually, they refined their communications to the point where Reiner only had to say "rubber bands" or Crystal to say "Buddy Rich" (the name of a famous drummer) and either would know the other was in trouble.

While comedy was what initially drew them together, it has taken a back seat over the years, according to Reiner. The late night split-screen telephone conversations that Harry and Sally share in the film as they compare notes on a movie they both saw were actually drawn from Reiner and Crystal's own habit of comparing notes by phone as they watched television.

"If we lived next door to each other we'd be connected with two paper cups and a string," Crystal joked.

While *When Harry Met Sally* turned out to be Reiner's biggest hit, it got the worst reviews of any picture he made. Reiner estimated the movie received only a 75-80 percent affirmative vote from the nation's critics. *Spinal Tap* did not get a single negative review that Reiner saw, while *Stand By Me*, *The Sure Thing* and *The Princess Bride* were about the same with 90 percent positive reviews.

Not only was the criticism negative, but *When Harry Met Sally* also attracted his first career backlash from an array of reviewers who charged him with poaching on Woody Allen's piece of Manhattan. However, the criticism put only a small dent in Reiner's growing reputation as a major director.

Reiner's next film was *Misery*, which was released in 1990 and based on the Stephen King novel of the same name. The period he spent between *All in the Family* and the release of *This is Spinal Tap* in 1984 provided the basis, Reiner said, for his identification with the subject of *Misery*, which is about a popular writer of romance novels named Paul Sheldon who is kidnapped by a demented fan at the moment he has killed off the fictional heroine who made him famous.

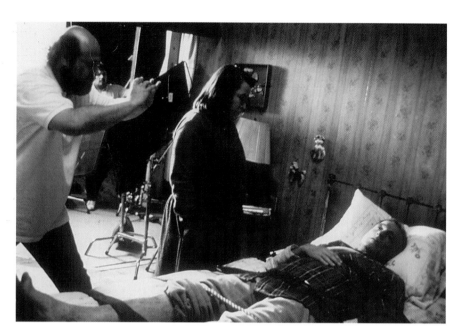

Reiner's next project was a dark comedy based on a novel by Stephen King about a writer kidnapped by a fanatical fan. Starring James Caan and Kathy Bates, *Misery* earned Bates an Oscar for Best Actress.

Reiner's experience was nothing as dramatic as what happens to the novelist, played by James Caan, who is held captive in a mountain cabin by a dreamy, homicidal fanatic played by Kathy Bates, who won an Academy Award for Best Actress for her role. Although he wasn't exactly a sex symbol, Reiner said he gained insight into what it's like for a creative person to go through the process of growing. "I went from being a sitcom actor to directing features," he said.

Reiner made the difficult transition, however, with eventual assistance from Lear, a family friend and the guy who hired him to play Meathead in *All in the Family*. Lear supplied the money to finance *Spinal Tap* when no one else thought the movie was worth making. He also provided the cash for Reiner's subsequent films. All proved to be profitable and drew wide critical approval.

Lear wouldn't reveal how much money he spent financing Reiner's films, although the budget for *The Princess Bride* was $17 million. Lear said his contributions on *Stand by Me* and *The Princess Bride* amounted to a total conviction that Reiner was going to make successful films. "I granted understanding," he said.

"Now, of course, my father's very proud of me," Rob said. Still, "I owe more to Norman than you might think. Norman is really responsible for giving me all the opportunities that I've had, not just as a filmmaker, but as an actor. He got me started with *All in the Family* and everything."

As Lear explained it, he never intended to finance Reiner's films, but it seemed he had the only film company in town that couldn't say no to him. In the case of *The Princess Bride*, Lear originally deemed it impossible to film because of its mixed elements. Lear offered bridge financing until and if a distributor could be found. The movie was in development at Embassy Communications, a production company Lear owned, before he sold it to Coca-Cola, which didn't want anything to do with the movie.

Lear's faith in Reiner's ability paid off big time. *This is Spinal Tap* cost $2.2 million to make and grossed almost $7 million at the domestic box office. *The Sure Thing* cost $4.5 million and grossed just under $20 million. And *Stand By Me* cost less than $8 million to make but brought in $53 million in the U.S. and about $75 million worldwide.

In his five previous movies, Reiner already had stretched beyond the boundaries of the laugh lines for which he and his father were famous and into some moderately serious and touching territory. *Misery* was seen as his most atypical movie yet. It's a campy, psychological thriller that depends on suspense as much as a Hitchcock film. The humor is anything but light, and in one painful scene, Bates' character breaks both of Sheldon's ankles with a sledgehammer.

It was Reiner's second adaptation of a Stephen King story after *Stand By Me*. *Misery* involved more alterations from the original, some of which were suggested by Warren Beatty, who once considered playing the role of Paul Sheldon. King gave his stamp of approval to the altered storyline in the film, going so far as to call Reiner's *Misery* his favorite of the 17 films and television adaptations that have been done of his books. At a private screening in Los Angeles, he walked up to the director and gave him a big hug.

Actress Lauren Bacall, who had a small role in *Misery*, praised Reiner for his versatility as a director.

"He's not into violence, that's not his theme, and he's not into a certain kind of slapstick comedy," she said. "He can do a little bit of everything, depending on the story he wants to tell. He's able to branch out and direct all kinds of movies, comedy or drama. If he's interested enough, he can do any-thing. Rob is one of those people and he's a rare director that reason. He doesn't go for the same stereotypical things."

By the early 1990s, critics were praising the warmth and light touch of Reiner's films, lending him an image as a leading good guy in a business famous for bad guys. "There's tremendous heart in all his films. And that's him. What you see onscreen is him," said Bruce Evans, co-author of the Oscar-nominated screenplay for *Stand By Me*.

With the record of five popular films behind him, Reiner no longer had to struggle to raise money or persuade anyone that he could point a camera in the right direction. Castle Rock, the production company he founded with Scheinman and three other partners in 1987 (and named after the fictional Oregon town in *Stand By Me*), was making four movies a year as well as several television shows, including *Seinfeld*. He was able to offer his father a job directing the film

Reiner has earned a reputation for working well with the actors on his films, by letting talents like Tom Cruise (seen here at work on the set of *A Few Good Men*) make each scene their own.

Sibling Rivalry, which Castle Rock financed.

But success brought its own set of problems for Reiner, who found it was much easier to climb the mountain than to stay on top. "Before, you had something to shoot for," he said. "You could see that goal. But once you get there you've got to create your own little goals and things. It's much more difficult."

Reiner's career as a director can be read in large part as a mirror of his personal life. He has shown a penchant for finding material that addressed his preoccupations, then works closely with screenwriters to tailor the scripts to his own point of view. But that process, said the writers and other associates, does not reflect the master-slave relationship often found in Hollywood.

Even a writer as independent and acerbic as Nora Ephron said about Reiner, "If one could do every movie with him, one would not have to think of needing to direct one's own."

Goldman, who wrote the screenplay for both *The Princess Bride* and *Misery*, said Reiner had the best script mind of anyone he had ever worked with. "He's a wonderful listener," Goldman said of Reiner. "He's willing to admit when he's wrong, and a lot of people aren't."

"All of Rob's films are somehow a reflection of what he's going through in his life," said Bruce Evans, who wrote *Stand By Me* with his partner Raynold Gideon. *The Sure Thing* was about dating; *Stand By Me* was about accepting his father; and when Billy Crystal's character in *When Harry and Sally* got married, Rob got married.

Evans and Gideon credited Reiner with giving the *Stand By Me* much of its quality and depth. He never tried to do anything behind their back. He would fight hard on something he didn't get, but in the end would shoot within four lines of the completed script. "He's the most honest director we ever worked with," Gideon said.

The line between Reiner and the story sometimes was a fine one. He described his identification with *Stand By Me* this way: "I was 12 years old in 1959. I know what it was like to be a depressed kid who didn't feel good about himself, who was concerned about whether or not his father loved him and trying to live up to his father."

Ephron had nothing but happy memories of her collaboration with Reiner on *When Harry Met Sally*, which resulted in an Oscar nomination for her. "We had a great time, with a surprising number of blips for a collaboration like this," she said. "He isn't like other directors. When he says he's going to do something, he does it. He's very decent. He's very down-to-earth. It's one phone call in ten that he doesn't place himself."

Reiner's talent as a director draws on his experience as an actor, according to those who have worked for him.

Bates, for example, said she felt like Reiner had been there before her. "The thing I liked most about him being such a good actor himself was I could always be sure the direction I was getting from him was accurate. He has such an unerring sense of timing and music and a great ear for the coloration of different speeches," she said.

As a director, Reiner would act through scenes as they were being written so that when they reached the rehearsal or shooting phase, the logistics would be worked out in his mind. He would never ask an actor to do something of which he was not capable.

"I would never ask an actor to make a transition I can't make in a scene," he said. "But if they are struggling with a transition or a moment, I can act it out for them. So I can give them that. They make it their own."

Peter Falk, a veteran television and movie actor who played the small role of the grandfatherly narrator in *The Princess Bride*, said, "You know, when an actor goes on the set, and the director has been an actor, immediately there is a connection, an ease. Rob has no compunctions about cutting through all the [nonsense]. He just says, 'Here, what about this?' And he can do it good and you get right to it and there's no problem. It was a wonderful experience, those four days."

Reiner, however, minimized his hands-on work with actors on the set. "A lot of actors don't like to get line readings, but I don't give line readings so much as to show them what I mean by acting it out for them. The best actors I've worked with don't mind that. They know that they're going to take it and make it their own."

Ephron called Reiner "a great actor." During the filming of *When Harry Met Sally*, Ephron said she desperately wanted him to play Harry. "In fact, I also wanted him to play Sally," she joked.

Even while he was carving out a successful career as a director, Reiner still did an occasional cameo. In *Postcards From the Edge*, for example, he played a fast-talking producer who oozes flattery on the strung-out Meryl Streep before asking her to take a drug test.

"It's fun if you only have to do it for a day," Reiner said of the infrequent acting jobs that he takes on.

The criticism that *When Harry Met Sally* was a Woody Allen wannabe movie brought out an exclamation point in Reiner's voice during one interview. The accusation bothered him deeply. "I mean, look at my work," he said, his voice rising. "It's not like I've made six Woody Allen films! Because I made a relationship film that takes place in New York about two upscale-type people who are closely connected to myself, I'm in Woody Allen area. So, nobody can make a film in New York about relationships unless they're Woody Allen? That's insane."

Then there was the criticism of *Sibling Rivalry*, the movie starring Kirstie Alley that his father directed for Castle Rock. "We got killed," he said of the reviews, "and it's a funny movie. You may not like the movie. But you can't go to this movie and say it's not funny. It's not something you can say. You go to the movie and people are screaming in the theater. That means it's funny whether you like it or not."

Does Reiner ever think where he would be had it not been for Lear, who, for example, not only bankrolled *Spinal Tap* to the tune of $3 million but came forward with the $9 million budget for *Stand By Me* when Columbia scuttled the project with only days to go before shooting was to begin?

"Who knows?" he said. "I always say, talent will win out. The cream rises. But maybe it would have taken a little longer. Certainly, he has been my main supporter all along."

Reiner remarried in May 1989, having met his wife,

Much of the funding for Reiner's films has come from producer Norman Lear. Since the days of *All in the Family*, Lear has recognized Reiner's talent and has provided millions in financial support for his projects.

Michele Singer, during the making of *When Harry Met Sally*. She was a photographer who, like her husband, always wanted to direct movies. In 1990, she directed her first music video.

People always ask whether he shows his father rough cuts of his films or asks for his advice. "I've never talked about that with my dad," he said. "I talk about a lot of things with him, but not usually this stuff. If you screen a film for an audience you can kind of tell what's lacking and what works. You don't really need people to tell you."

In 1992, Reiner released *A Few Good Men*. It was the first time as a director that he had to deal with megastars such as Tom Cruise, Jack Nicholson and Demi Moore in one of his films. Reiner was nervous about the prospect of dealing with such big egos with a $40-million plus budget on the line. But it turned out to be the easiest of his movies to date. *A Few Good Men*, Reiner's seventh film, earned him another nomination from the Directors Guild of America for Best Director award, as well as an Academy Award for Best Picture.

The stars credited the relaxed, professional atmosphere of the set to Reiner's fanatical approach to preparation for each scene. It didn't hurt that Reiner is strong-willed, physically imposing, and commands a lot of attention. "There's usually not a lot of acting out on the set," he said.

Actor Kevin Bacon said Reiner created an atmosphere where everyone wanted to do their best to make a great movie. Bacon, who played the prosecutor who takes on defense lawyer Cruise, said Reiner began each day of shooting with a clear idea of what he wanted to accomplish. He planned out his shots well, made sure the actors had rehearsed, and discussed with them how they fit into the big picture.

"We enjoyed the process of making the movie," he said. "It was like, 'bam, bam, bam.' Let's work. Let's get it done.

Everyone felt we were in good hands. That's the key to having a successful cast."

Moore said Reiner's relentless attention to detail and painstaking preparing were also important factors in the success of the movie.

"There is nothing better you can do for yourself, for your actors and for your entire company than be extremely prepared," said Moore.

That's exactly what Reiner did. He worked on the script for several months with screenwriter Aaron Sorkin, who adapted his own Broadway play. Reiner insisted on building up Cruise's character's conflict with his father and even changing a major plot device to build suspense.

Sorkin was so happy with the changes that he went back and rewrote the script for his play to reflect the changes in his movie script.

"I spent many months with him [Reiner] before the first day of shooting," Sorkin said. "And that intense, passionate work on the script for me is Rob Reiner directing the movie. You want to be good for him. Everybody really loves the guy and we all want him to win coach-of-the-year."

The success of *A Few Good Men* turned out to be a watershed event for Castle Rock Entertainment, the independent film company started by Reiner and friends a few years earlier. Through the movie company was responsible for hits such as *City Slickers* and other profitable movies directed by Reiner, Castle Rock had a series of disappointments, including *Mr. Saturday Night*, *Year of the Comet*, and *Late for Dinner*, and *Honeymoon in Vegas* was only a modest success.

In *A Few Good Men*, Cruise plays Daniel Kaffee, a young, smooth-talking Navy lawyer fresh out of Harvard Law School. Kaffee is overshadowed by the reputation of his esteemed lawyer father. One of the reasons Reiner

The 1992 film *A Few Good Men* marked the first time Reiner would work with mega-stars like Tom Cruise, Jack Nicholson, and Demi Moore. The movie centers on a Navy trial and earned Reiner a Best Picture Oscar.

chose to make *A Few Good Men* was because he saw himself in the Cruise character.

"The struggle that Kaffee goes through, trying to extricate himself from the shadow of his famous father, is something that I know pretty well," Reiner said.

Reiner's next effort, released in 1994, was *North*. Based on a novella written by Alan Zweibel, the movie is about an eleven-year-old boy who doesn't get along with his parents and decides to conduct a worldwide search to find replacement parents who would appreciate him.

In the mid-1980s, Zweibel, who was a writer for *Saturday Night Live*, sent a copy of the book to Reiner, who had once hosted the show. Reiner said he would like to direct it as a movie some day but went off to do another fairytale, *The Princess Bride*, and Zweibel became involved with another television show.

The two kept in touch. One day in 1992, Zweibel was talking to Reiner and the director asked what had happened to the little novella. One thing led to another and soon Reiner agreed to take on the project.

The movie was not well received, either by critics or at the box office. After a string a hits, it was Reiner's first true flop.

With the harsh words ringing in his ears, Reiner had lunch one day with actor John Travolta. The once hot actor's career had fallen into the doldrums. But Travolta came up with a philosophical way of looking at the situation, which struck a chord with Reiner.

"He said 'I wasn't that great then and I'm not that bad now,'" Reiner recalled. "It's true. They build you up, then they tear you down. *North* was not that bad. It was a slight little fable.

"I think it was my time to get hammered," Reiner said of the review for *North*. "It's probably not my best film, but there are a lot of funny things in it. Distance will tell."

Reiner bounced back stronger than ever in 1995 *The American President*, about a widowed president (Michael Douglas) struggling to balance his presidency with his newfound love life in the form of Annette Benning.

In some ways, it was Reiner's most difficult film as he tried to blend politics, romance and comedy into one package. As most filmmakers will say, mix in romance and comedy is difficult enough. But throw in politics and try to make it serious and realistic and you have an impossible formula.

Somehow, Reiner managed to pull it off. The movie touches a nerve about privacy.

"I think it's important that we become a more informed

public, and that we vote based on what we know about a person's positions and ability to do the job," Reiner said. "It shouldn't matter whether or not somebody had an affair—unless it involves violence or incest or some other criminal activity. With public officials the public may have some right to know about personal finances, since this could reflect on how they conduct public finances. Otherwise, the person is not for public consumption."

Reiner's next film was *Ghosts of Mississippi*, released in 1996. It was his first movie based on historical fact. He was religious about adhering to historical accuracy in the film.

Ghosts of Mississippi is the true-life drama of how a relentless young Mississippi district attorney named Bobby DeLaughter (Alec Baldwin) did what his colleagues said was impossible—convict white supremacist Byron De La Beckwith (James Woods) for the murder of civil rights leader Medgar Evers 31 years later, even after two earlier trials ended with hung juries.

It was a story that was with Reiner much of his life. Reiner was a student at Beverly Hills High School when Evers was shot in the back as he returned home from work one night in Jackson, Mississippi, in 1963.

"It was something that was certainly discussed in my house," Reiner said of the assassination. "I remember it was very, very shocking because nothing like this had happened before. Here was a man who was very moderate, intelligent, well-spoken person. He was not a rabble-rouser. He was trying in a very decent, lawful way to get some civil rights for his fellow man. The idea that he would be gunned down for that, in his driveway, in front of his wife and children, was very disturbing."

As the turbulence of the 1960s unfolded from that point, Reiner's family, like others, often got caught up in the

Ghosts of Mississippi, released in 1996, was Reiner's first historically-based film. The story centers on the efforts of young district attorney to convict white supremacist Byron De La Beckwith in the murder of civil rights activist Medgar Evers.

events. He remembers his father taking part in the anti-Vietnam War protests of the early 1970s and his mother organizing the group "Another Mother for Peace" and designing its famous "War is Hazardous to Children and Other Livings Things" poster.

Reiner never lost his connection to the activism of the 1960s and when he saw DeLaughter's efforts to reopen the Evers investigation on the news, he thought it would make an interesting movie.

Ghosts of Mississippi tells how DeLaughter, a white man from an Old South family, sees his personal life disintegrate under the pressure of his effort to convict

Byron de La Beckwith, which is met at first with skepticism from Evers' wife, Myrlie.

Reiner felt the same thing when he decided to produce and direct the film. He worked closely with Myrlie Evers and he thought initially she had some legitimate misgivings about how the movie would turn out.

"I think every black person in this country, on the surface of things, might have misgivings about a white person portraying some aspect of their reality," Reiner said. "But if you realize his motives come from a very good, decent, compassionate place, then those misgivings melt away. And in the case of Myrlie, that's exactly what happened."

Just in case they hadn't, though, Reiner said he agreed Castle Rock Entertainment would pull the plug if Mrs. Evers-Williams felt the story wasn't being told accurately.

Woods said Reiner's passion for making a great movie was obvious. "I honestly believe that if someone could have looked into the future and said this movie wouldn't make any money, as a professional filmmaker and as financially responsible as he is, I think Rob would have made it either way," Woods said. "He would have gotten a handheld camera and hired some unknown actors and he would go and tell this story because it's so important and it meant so much to him."

Woods said an incident that happened during the making of the film made it clear why Reiner felt so strongly. A little black girl wanted to know about the movie that was bring made. He told it was about Medgar Evers. She didn't know whom he was talking about.

"That's why Rob put on their earth," Woods said. "To answer her question."

Reiner's next film, and the last one before a major career shift, was *The Story of Us*, a social comedy with a message.

The he-she relationship yarn starred Bruce Willis and Michelle Pfeiffer, who play a married couple with two kids but who are at odds and near divorce. She's fed up with taking care of their "third child"—her husband— and frustrated with being the "designated driver" in their relationship. He wants spontaneity and can't get it. He wants less drama and more comedy, and ultimately less responsibility. The film is somewhat like a sequel to *When Harry Met Sally*, only about 15 years and lots of arguments later.

Reiner said that one of themes of the movie is that husbands and fathers must learn how to take over more duties at home, a lesson he learned from experience.

"That is true," he said. "For the most part, women are the caretakers and they are smarter, and that's why they're doing that job of taking care of the home and a career, because if men had to do both, both would be a mess."

By 1997, however, Reiner's interests were turning away from Hollywood and toward a more important vocation. At the peak of his popularity as a director, Reiner temporarily shelved his Hollywood career in 1997 to direct himself in what he called the most passionate role of his career: to spearhead a first-of-its kind children's initiative.

CELEBRATE!

Reiner's work outside of filmmaking continues to keep him busy. His tireless efforts to promote a cigarette tax that would benefit childhood development programs led to the passage of California's Proposition 10 in 1998.

Chapter 6

Meathead for President?

IT WAS LIGHTS, camera, action for actor/director Rob Reiner, as he stepped to a bank of microphones in the courtyard of Children's Institute International one day in the Spring of 1998.

"Proposition 10 could be the most important law in the history of U.S. childcare," Reiner said in announcing a November California ballot initiative that would add a 50-cent tax on a package of cigarettes and generate $700 million annually for early childhood development programs. "I'm hoping this will mark the beginning of a sea change in how we deal with children in this country. Passage in California will give this legs for passage in every other state."

On the heels of a string of award nominations in the early 1990s, Reiner put his film career entirely on hold to push for the California Children and Families Initiative. The tax was expected to generate hundreds of millions of dollars for early childcare, intervention programs for at-risk children, and smoking prevention programs for pregnant women, parents and teenagers.

Reiner spent $2 million of his own money to help collect 1.2 million signatures to qualify for the ballot. He hoped to raise another $3 million to $4 million more from other sources, including friends, businesses and foundations.

For Reiner, the prospect of passing Proposition 10 came only after months of solid, 50-hour weeks that included policy meetings, legislative testimony, and public appearance from Rotary Clubs to Lion's Club luncheons. Before that, it was trips to New York, Washington, Atlanta and to every corner of the Golden State to learn as much as he could about existing state and federal children's policy and programs.

"It's actually astonishing how much Rob knows about every aspect of this issue," said Gionvanna Stark, executive director of California's child-development policy advisory committee, during the campaign. "Most Hollywood types know about the surface issues but don't understand the underlying policy implications. Rob has become a full-fledged expert."

Along the way, Reiner was criticized by some for supporting Proposition 10. Opponents said he was personally misguided for designing an initiative they said would create an unneeded government bureaucracy. The anti-tax group, funded mostly by the tobacco industry, seemed to be tapping into general disgust with government programs.

Reiner's interest in childcare issues was not new or event recent at the time. His intense curiosity dated back 20 years to therapy he underwent after a breakup with ex-wife Penny Marshall.

Reiner realized in that process that society needs to think more deeply about how children are raised and what effect the earliest years of development have on later behavior.

The former bohemian exchanged his blue jeans and flannel shirts for business suits and wingtips. Remarried with young children of his own, Reiner four years earlier began a nationwide campaign to raise consciousness on how important a child's first three years are. The campaign began in his living room with discussions among key childcare specialists that included Vice President Al Gore. "We talked to all the top child experts in this country," recalled Reiner. "It's very clear that . . . children who are neglected on abused during this period are much more likely to become troubled adults who cost millions in law enforcement, welfare, and incarceration."

Reiner's involvement blossomed into discussions with President Clinton, commercial and public television campaigns, national magazine spreads, and a permanent foundation. Reiner also produced a primetime television special on the subject.

"Public policy is a completely different mind-set than Hollywood," said Reiner. "In show biz, you are just making up stuff, trying to please, producing fantasy and laughs. With this initiative, this is serious and there is much more at stake in affecting millions of people in a very real way."

Interestingly enough, Reiner discovered much of the information after his own sons were past the age of three. Instinctively, he and his wife tried to spend at least four

Here, Reiner and wife Michele meet with President Clinton to discuss child development programs. Reiner's work has given rise to numerous public information campaigns on both commercial and public TV.

or five nights a week reading to their sons.

"We try to spend as much time with them as possible," he said. "Nobody died saying 'I should have spent more time at the office.'"

Unlike other celebrities who attach themselves to an issue in a superficial way, sort of like a flavor-of-the-month approach, Reiner devoted all his energies to the cause. He didn't make a movie for two years and sacrificed more than $10 million in potential earnings to start the foundation, press for better childcare, educate the public and chair the ballot campaign.

His level of dedication took some people by surprise.

"I have seen a lot of Hollywood celebrities put their name or face on an issue, but never have I seen anyone immerse themselves as deeply or passionately as Rob Reiner," said Mary Emmons, director of Children's Institute International, an organization dedicated to prevention of child abuse and neglect. "His stature and commitment have heightened the profile of these issues."

Sitting front and center at a state hearing one day in 1997 as he built support for the initiative, Reiner was both in and out of his element. Preaching in a booming voice, he lectured the legislators about nurturing children from conception to kindergarten as he testified in favor of Proposition 10.

Such stimulation "is vitamins, it is food, it is nutrition for the brain," bellowed Reiner.

He told the panel how the $700 million would be spent: the state commission overseeing the program would take 20 percent of the revenues to pay for statewide programs, including a tobacco education program, and professional staff. The remaining 80 percent would be given to counties based on their proportion of births in the previous year. A network of volunteer commissions would be set up in each county to distribute the wealth to new and existing programs of their choice. Options under the initiative would vary from prenatal nutrition and day-care programs to filling gaps in child health care and cosmetic violence prevention systems.

Los Angeles County, for example, would receive about $176 million the first year. Orange County would get about $50 million while Ventura County would net about $12 million.

On Feb. 4, 1997, Reiner appeared before the nation's governors to pitch his belief about the importance of the way children under three are brought up. He urged the governors to shift their financial resources to make sure enough funding would be available for the kids.

"I know how to put on a show," he told them. "It's what I do. I put on shows."

Republican Gov. Pete Wilson of California praised Reiner's presentation to the group. "In the six years I have been attending these meetings, I have never seen a more impressive presentation," Wilson said.

James B. Hunt, the Democrat governor from North Carolina, agreed. "Mr. Reiner, you are absolutely right," he said. "Thank you for pointing us in the right direction."

In the end, the NGA named early childhood development its top priority for the future. It was another victory for Reiner as he drummed up support for early childhood development programs.

By then, his campaign had already lined up a host of corporate sponsors, including IBM and AT&T. Foundations were on board as well, including the MacArthur and Theresa & H. John Heinz III.

Then Reiner went to the American Broadcasting Company and asked for an hour of airtime to do a special focusing on early childhood development. He promised to make it entertaining and informative. They agreed.

Reiner's documentary, *I Am Your Child*, debuted on April 21 that year. Starring Tom Hanks, Robin Williams, Colin Powell, Arnold Swartzenegger, Bruce Willis, Demi Moore,

After an appeal to the nation's governors to provide more funds for childhood development, Reiner was praised by California Governor Pete Wilson (seen here) for his presentation.

Rosie O'Donnell and other show business luminaries, the program drew amazing support from the media. ABC hyped the special all week on its *Good Morning America* show, while *Newsweek* produced a special issue devoted entirely to early childhood development. A free brochure for parents, and a video and CD-Rom for new parents also were part of the package developed by Reiner.

After Proposition 10 passed in November 1998, the commission was criticized early on for not getting money out quickly enough. Like most new government programs, it endured terrible growing pains during its first year.

Unlike a movie set, where the director has complete control of everything that happens, being one member of a seven-member commission has limited power. Reiner had to adjust to building a consensus in all major decisions. It took time but he eventually mastered the technique.

Even while he was working on behalf of early childhood programs, Reiner maintained his connection to Hollywood. In October 1999, he was enshrined in the Hollywood Walk of Fame with a star right next to the one dedicated to his father.

More than 300 people, including Carl Reiner, gathered on Hollywood Boulevard to witness the unveiling of the walk's 2,146th star.

"I'm in a good place next to my father," Rob told the cheering crowd.

Carl Reiner said it was gratifying to see his son honored. He joked that the two of them could show up at the Walk on weekdays and polish each other's stars.

As the younger Reiner approached the podium to make some remarks, someone in the audience yelled, "We love you Meathead."

Reiner shook his head. "I get Meathead every time," he lamented.

If the child advocacy world was thrilled to have a celebrity in its midst, the film world was mostly indifferent. "Nobody in Los Angeles, in this industry, knows what I do," he said without complaint. "Nobody knows about the meetings where I spend eight, nine hours in a room talking about policy, which is what I've done on a monthly basis for three years."

In 1999, Reiner received perhaps the most enduring praise for his work—a star on Hollywood's Walk of Fame, right next to his father's.

Reiner will hold his post on the commission until 2005. His sabbatical from Hollywood does raise the issue of whether he is more likely to return to movies or follow Ronald Reagan's footsteps and commit to politics. Former actor Reagan abandoned Hollywood in the 1970s, became governor of California and was elected President of the United States in 1980.

"I kid him that he's kind of a politician now," said Al Gore. "He would put the emphasis in 'kind of,' so at least for now that stays in the kidding category. But if he ever wanted to do something [in politics] I'm sure he would have a lot of supporters. My sense is that he's sort of primarily focused on the results, and he getting a lot of results this way."

Asked if anyone has suggested that he has been away from film too long, Reiner booms, "Anyone? How about every person that I meet? My wife is killing me to go back!"

By 2002, several scripts had Reiner's interest, although he refused to talk about them specifically. He planned to starts shooting one of them that year. But there were other reasons to give more attention to his old job as director. Submerged in his Prop. 10 work, he was surprised and infuriated when he saw the Castle Rock release of *Proof of Life* in 2001.

"Meg Ryan smokes throughout the movie," he said, shaking his head. "There's no reason for it."

While Commissioner Reiner can proudly point to a 35 percent drop in cigarette sales to minors in the first year after the passage of Proposition 10, filmmaker Reiner recognizes that cinema has done more to glamorize smoking that the tobacco industry can ever hope to.

Now if someone is to light up frivolously on a Castle Rock set, Reiner wants the opportunity to talk the director or actor out of that choice. In early 2001, he met Ryan Gosling, a 21-year-old actor who playing the role of a teenage murderer in a Castle Rock film directed by Barbet Schroeder. Reiner took a hard line with the young actor, who smoked heavily as part of his role.

"Making this choice could conceivably get someone to start smoking, and ultimately kill them. I just wanted you to know that," he told Gosling, who, nevertheless, held his ground and puffed away in the movie.

Reiner later found out that Gosling is a Mormon who doesn't smoke, drink, or swear. "He's as clean-living as they come, and he did a tremendous about of research into this character. So, we're not going to be censors, but if I were directing this film, I wouldn't let him smoke," he said.

Soon, Reiner will be a director again. He'll be back in control of a little world of his own making. There will be no smoking. And no committees. And no show of hands.

"It's fun, first of all," he said of directing. But he has no plans to abandon his other world, despite its never-ending meetings and frustrating bureaucratic red tape. "I didn't know what I was getting into," he admitted. "But that's OK because it's a tremendous opportunity to get things done. It's also a tremendous responsibility. You can't just walk away. I'm not going to."

1945 Born in New York City on March 6 to Carl and Estelle Reiner

1967 Kicked out of UCLA for skipping classes

1971 Begins role as Mike Stivic on *All in the Family*; marries Penny Marshall

1979 *All in the Family* comes to an end; Reiner and Marshall are divorced

1987 Co-founds Castle Rock Entertainment

1989 Marries photographer Michele Singer

1990 Son Jake is born

1993 Son Nick is born

1997 Daughter Romy is born; forms the I Am Your Child Foundation; *I Am Your Child* airs on ABC

1998 Spearheads campaign for passage of Proposition 10 in California, which passes

1967   *Enter Laughing*
Actor

1970   *Hall of Anger*
Actor

Where's Poppa?
Actor

1971-1979   *All in the Family* (TV)
Actor

1971   *Summertree*
Actor

1973   *The Super* (TV)
Producer

1975   *How Come Nobody's on Our Side?*
Actor

1977   *Fire Sale*
Actor

1978   *Free Country* (TV)
Producer

More Than Friends (TV)
Producer

1979   *The T.V. Show* (TV)
Producer

1981   *Likely Stories*
Actor

1982   *Million Dollar Infield*
Actor

1984   *This is Spinal Tap*
Actor
Director

1985   *The Sure Thing*
Director

1986   *Stand By Me*
Director

1987   *The Princess Bride*
Director
Producer

       Throw Mama From the Train
Actor

1989   *When Harry Met Sally*
Director
Producer

1990   *Misery*
Director
Producer

       Postcards from the Edge
Actor

1991   *Spirit of '76*
Actor

       Morton and Hayes (TV)
Producer

1992   *A Few Good Men*
Director
Producer

1993   *Sleepless in Seattle*
Actor

1994   *North*
Director
Producer

       Bullets Over Broadway
Actor

       Mixed Nuts
Actor

1995   *Bye-Bye Love*
Actor

       The American President
Director
Producer

1996 *The First Wives Club*
Actor

For Better or Worse
Actor

Trigger Happy
Actor

Ghosts of Mississippi
Director
Producer

1997 *I Am Your Child* (TV)
Director

1998 *Primary Colors*
Actor

1999 *The Story of Us*
Actor
Director
Producer

Edtv
Actor
Director

2001 *The Majestic*
Actor (voice)

1973-74 Emmy: Best Supporting Actor in a Comedy Series, *All in the Family*

1977-78 Emmy: Best Supporting Actor in a Comedy Series, *All in the Family*

1993 MTV Movie Award, *A Few Good Men*; American Cinematheque Award

1997 Honorary People's Choice Award: Special achievement tribute for his 30 years in television and film

The Directors. American Film Institute, 1999. Videocassette.

McCrohan, Donna. *Archie & Edith, Mike & Gloria*. New York: Workman Publishing, 1987.

Adato, Allison. "The Power of One: the Education of Meathead," *The Los Angeles Times*, Jan. 20, 2002.

The Directors. American Film Institute, 1999. Videocassette.

McCrohan, Donna. *Archie & Edith, Mike & Gloria*. New York: Workman Publishing, 1987.

Gilbert, Matthew. "Rob Reiner Grows into Success." *The Boston Globe*, Dec. 11, 1992.

Mitchell, Sean. "The Sweet Misery that Fame Brings." *The Los Angeles Times*, Nov. 25, 1990.

"Rob Reiner." *Personalities and Profiles: The Playboy Interview Collection* CD-Rom. Originally published November 1985.

Wood, Daniel B. "Parlaying a Career into a Crusade," *Christian Science Monitor*, October 20, 1998.

http://us.imdb.com/Name?Reiner,+Rob
  [Internet Movie Database]

http://www.eonlne.com/Facts/People/Bio/0,128,153,00.html
  [E! Online]

http://www.canoe.ca/JamMoviesArtistsR/reiner.html
  [Jam!]

http://castle-rock.warnerbros.com/cmp/html/aboutcre.html
  [Castle Rock Entertainment]

http://www.nrdc.org/reference/profiles/prorein.sap
  [National Resources Defense Council]

ABC, 32
  and *I Am Your Child,* 73, 76-77
Academy Award, for *A Few Good Men,* 62
Academy Award nominations
  for *Stand by Me,* 42, 56
  for *When Harry Met Sally,* 49
ACVO/Embassy, and *This is Spinal Tap,* 38-39
Allen, Woody, 53, 60
Alley, Kirstie, in *Sibling Rivalry,* 60
All in the Family (TV), 8, 26-32
  and end of show, 35
  impact of, 30
  and Lear, 26, 29, 54, 55
  Reiner as Meathead in, 27-28, 29-30, 37
  Reiner's lessons from, 29-30
  story of, 26, 28
  success of, 26-27, 28-29, 30
American President, The, 64-65
Arnez, Desi, 22

Bacall, Lauren, in *Misery,* 56
Bacon, Kevin, in *A Few Good Men,* 62-63
Baldwin, Alec, in *Ghosts of Mississippi,* 66
Barrett, Rona, 22-23
Bates, Kathy, 59
  in *Misery,* 54, 55-56
Beatty, Warren, 56
Benning, Annette, in *The American President,* 65
Beverly Hillbillies, The (TV), 22
Beverly Hills High School, 20, 66
Bishop, Larry, 20
Brooks, Albert, 20
Brooks, Harvey, 21-22
Brooks, Mel, 16

Caan, James, in *Misery,* 54
Caesar, Sid, 16
California Children and Families Commission, 7-8, 13, 78, 80
California Children and Families Initiative (Proposition 13), 8, 10-13, 71-78, 80

Cass, Mama, 21
Castle Rock Entertainment, 56-57, 81
  and *A Few Good Men,* 63
  and *Ghosts of Mississippi,* 68
  and *Proof of Life,* 80-81
  and *Sibling Rivalry,* 60
  and *When Harry Met Sally,* 49-50
City Slickers, 63
Clinton, Bill, 73
Coca, Imogene, 16
Columbia Studios, and *Stand by Me,* 44-45, 60
Committee, The, 21-22, 25
Cruise, Tom, in *A Few Good Men,* 62, 63
Crystal, Billy
  Reiner's friendship with, 41, 51-53
  in *This is Spinal Tap,* 38
  in *When Harry Met Sally,* 49, 51, 58
Cusack, John, in *The Sure Thing,* 39, 41

Davis, Gray, 13
Directors Guild of America nomination
  for *A Few Good Men,* 62
  for *Stand by Me,* 42
  for *When Harry Met Sally,* 49
Douglas, Michael, in *The American President,* 65
Dreyfuss, Richard, 20, 51

Embassy Communications, 55
Emmons, Mary, 75
Emmy Award, for *All in the Family,* 31
Enter Laughing (play), 19
Ephron, Nora, 57
  and *When Harry Met Sally,* 50, 51, 58, 59
Evans, Bruce, 58
  and *Stand by Me,* 56, 58
Evers, Medgar, and *Ghosts of Mississippi,* 66-68
Evers, Myrlie, 68

Falk, Peter, 59
  in *The Princess Bride,* 46, 59
Feldman, Corey, in *Stand by Me,* 43

Few Good Men, A, 62-64
    awards and nominations for, 62
    budget for, 62
    cast for, 62-63
    script for, 63
    shooting of, 62-63
    story of, 63-64
    success of, 63
Free Country (TV), 32

Ghosts of Mississippi, 66-68
    cast for, 66
    story of, 66, 67-68
Gideon, Raynold, and *Stand by Me,* 58
Glen Campbell Show, The (TV), 25
Goldman, William, 58
    and *Misery,* 58
    and *The Princess Bride,* 45-46, 58
Gomer Pyle USMC (TV), 22
Gore, Al, 12, 73, 80
Gore, Tipper, 9
Gosling, Ryan, 81
Gottlieb, Carl, and *The Glen Campbell
    Show,* 25
Griffith, Andy, 32

Hanks, Tom, in *I Am Your Child,* 76
Headmaster (TV), 32
Henderson, Alan, 11-12
Hollywood Walk of Fame, 78
Honeymoon in Vegas, 63
Hunt, James B., 76

I Am Your Child (TV), 73, 76-77
"I Am Your Child" foundation, 10, 73

Joplin, Janis, 22, 30

King, Stephen
    and *Misery,* 53, 56
    and *Stand by Me,* 42, 56

Late for Dinner, 63
Lavern & Shirley (TV), 31-32, 33
Lear, Norman
    and *All in the Family,* 26, 29, 54, 55
    and *The Princess Bride,* 55

and Reiner's humor, 16-17
and *Stand by Me,* 44, 55, 56, 60
and *The Sure Thing,* 40-41, 55
and *This is Spinal Tap,* 38-39, 40,
    54, 55, 60

McElwaine, Guy, 45
Marshall, Penny (ex-wife), 15, 30-32,
    33, 50, 73
Martin, Steve, 26
Miller, Steve, 22
Misery, 53-54
    cast for, 54, 55-56
    script for, 58
    story of, 53-54, 56
Mishkin, Phil, 32
Mocumentary, 37
    See also This is Spinal Tap
Moore, Demi
    in *A Few Good Men,* 62, 63
    in *I Am Your Child,* 76
Mothers-in-Law, The (TV), 22-23
Mr. Saturday Night, 63

Nicholson, Jack, 30
    in *A Few Good Men,* 62
No Exit (play), 19-20
North, 64-65

O'Connor, Carroll, in *All in the Family,*
    26, 29
O'Donnell, Rosie, in *I Am Your Child,*
    77

Pfeiffer, Michelle, in *The Story of Us,*
    69
Postcards From the Edge, 60
Powell, Colin, in *I Am Your Child,* 76
Princess Bride, The, 11, 45-47, 50, 65
    budget for, 45, 55
    cast for, 46, 59
    financing for, 55
    reviews of, 53
    story of, 45-47
Proof of Life, 80-81

Redford, Robert, 47

Reiner, Annie (sister), 9, 16
Reiner, Carl (father), 15-16, 17-20, 26,
    30, 33-35, 42, 46, 55, 56-57, 58, 60,
    62, 63-64, 67, 78
Reiner, Estelle (mother), 15, 19, 26, 30
Reiner, Rob
    and activism of 1960s, 66-67
    as actor, 22, 26-32, 34-35, 39, 54,
        55, 58-60
    and baseball, 41-42
    birth of, 15
    childhood of, 15-19, 34, 58
    children of, 9, 73-74
    and comedy, 20-22, 25, 33-34
    directorial style of, 41, 56, 57-59,
        62-63
    and divorce, 32-33, 35, 50, 73
    and early childhood development
        programs, 7-13, 69, 71-78, 80-81
    and early interest in show business,
        19-20
    education of, 19, 20, 29-30
    family of, 15-20, 26, 30, 33-35, 42,
        46, 55, 56-57, 58, 60, 62, 63-64,
        67, 78
    and first director's job, 37-39
    and honors and awards, 31, 42, 49,
        56, 62, 78
    and interest in directing, 27, 29-30,
        37
    marriages of, 30, 60, 62. *See also*
        Marshall, Penny; Singer, Michele
    and sense of humor, 16-17, 19
    and smoking, 8, 10-13, 71-78, 80
    on success, 57
    as writer, 25-26, 32
Roos, Mike, 10
Ryan, Meg
    in *Proof of Life,* 80
    in *When Harry Met Sally,* 49

Scheinmen, Andrew
    and Castle Rock, 56
    and *When Harry Met Sally,* 46, 50
Schroeder, Barbet, 81
Seinfeld (TV), 56
Sessions, The, 20

Sibling Rivalry, 56-57, 60
Simon, Neil, 16
Singer, Michele (wife), 10, 60, 62,
    73-74, 80
Smothers Brothers, 25-26
Smothers Brothers Show, The (TV),
    25-26
Sorkin, Aaron, and *A Few Good Men,*
    63
Stand by Me, 11, 42-45
    budget for, 42
    cast for, 42, 43, 44
    financing for, 55, 60
    nominations for, 42, 56
    reviews of, 53
    script for, 56, 58
    story of, 42-43, 45, 56, 58
    studio for, 44-45
    success of, 56
Stanton, Harry Dean, 30
Stapleton, Jean, in *All in the Family,*
    26
Stark, Gionvanna, 72
"Starting Points" report (Carnegie
    Corporation), 9-10
Story of Us, The, 68-69
Streep, Meryl, in *Postcards from the
    Edge,* 60
Struthers, Sally, in *All in the Family,*
    26
Sure Thing, The, 39-41, 42
    cast for, 39, 41
    financing for, 40-41, 55
    reviews of, 53
    story of, 39-40, 58
    success of, 41, 65
Swartzenegger, Arnold, in *I Am Your
    Child,* 76

That Girl (TV), 22
This is Spinal Tap, 37-39, 53
    cast for, 38, 39
    financing for, 38-39, 40, 54, 55, 60
    and Reiner's father, 42
    reviews of, 53
    story of, 38, 39
    success of, 37, 55

"Three Haircuts, The" (skit), 42

Tobacco, and California Children and Families Initiative, 8, 10-13, 71-78, 80

Travolta, John, 65

TV Show, The (TV), 32

University of California at Los Angeles, 20

Vietnam War, 20, 67

When Harry Met Sally, 11, 49-53, 69
    cast for, 49, 51-53, 58
    nominations for, 49
    reviews of, 53, 60

    script for, 50, 58
    story of, 49, 50, 58

Williams, Robin, in *I Am Your Child,* 76

Willis, Bruce
    in *I Am Your Child,* 76
    in *The Story of Us,* 69

Wilson, Pete, 76

Woods, James, in *Ghosts of Mississippi,* 66, 68

Year of the Comet, 63

Young, Robert, 32

Zuniga, Daphne, in *The Sure Thing,* 39

Zweibel, Alan, and *North,* 64-65

Picture Credits

Joe Ferry is a veteran journalist who has worked for several newspapers in the Philadelphia suburbs since 1977. He is a graduate of West Catholic High School and Eastern College. He has also written about actress Helen Hunt for Chelsea House. Mr. Ferry lives in Sellersville, Bucks County, Pennsylvania with his wife, three children and two dogs.